Broadly
Speaking

Broadly Speaking

100 Years of Wisecracks, Insights, Retorts & Wisdom **from Women in Comedy**

Compiled by Barbara Darko with Rob Shaeffer
Princeton Architectural Press, New York

Comedy Needs Women

Across time and across the globe, women
in comedy have put in the work, paid their
dues, and let fly a wealth of pointed jokes
and humorous insights. They've poked fun at,
made fodder of, crossed wits over, and set up
punchlines about everything and everyone,
including themselves. Their perspective has
only sharpened the barbs and amplified
the big ideas they've let loose on the world.
As women's roles have evolved, especially
over the last hundred-odd years, so too has
their comedy, breaking out from themes
of hearth and home to cover femininity, fame,
and fortune; feminism, philosophy, and,
yes, the f-word; coming full circle to address
comedy as a genre, a delivery mechanism,
and a job. ✳ Funny women, by presence
alone and with their words, spotlight the
disparity between their lack of representation
in mainstream comedy and the necessity

of their inclusion. Intentionally or not, a female comic broadens the scope of comedy with a crack about the latest problematic politician— or bit about taking off her bra—as she wins over an intimate club or a jam-packed theater. Her words might be a well-honed weapon, or perhaps they are armor, or both. Maybe due to media fatigue or the rise of fake news, it is easier than ever to see the glimmer of truth, the silliness, and the sarcasm that female comics offer as a beacon—a bastion, even.

✳ And rest assured: brighter days are ahead for women in comedy. It's clear from the increasing visibility and diversity of the people who are given a platform to speak to the spectrum of female, and by extension human, experiences. This progress rests on the shoulders of the great women comics who paved the way. Phyllis Diller [85, 127], Joan Rivers [47, 120], and Betty White [125, 128] (may she outlive us all) gave us self-deprecation; Lily Tomlin [61, 126] (better known to those of us of a certain generation as one Ms. Frizzle) gave us irony, and, along with Gina Yashere [108, 129], Lea DeLaria [50, 70], and Ellen DeGeneres [137], paved the way for the next generation of queer comics; and the likes of Moms Mabley [122] and Whoopi Goldberg [13] broadened the talent pool, challenging notions of what women in comedy look like. ✳ Thankfully, representation is on the rise. Leslie Jones's [36, 107, 144] sidesplitting 2010 special *Problem Child*, for example, is proof that she'd been funny long before she broke onto the *Saturday Night Live* stage in 2014, building upon a career that began in the late eighties. Jones's *SNL* debut came the same year that Amber Ruffin [54], known for her work on *Late Night with Seth Meyers*, became the first black female late-night writer. (Ruffin once told the *Chicago Tribune*, "I love Whoopi Goldberg. I love to think that I'm a lot like her...on paper"—and she is, in our book!) In 2018, Nora Lum, better known by her stage name, Awkwafina [60], was the first East Asian American *SNL* host since Lucy Liu's appearance on the show eighteen years earlier, inspiring her to aim for the same star and stage. As major platforms invest in specials and projects by and for women, so immigrant, LGBTQ+, otherwise-abled, and underrepresented women are also uplifted and the medium increasingly speaks to and reflects everyone. ✳ Needless to say, comedy is necessary no matter the political climate, but it is particularly vital during times of upheaval and unrest. Through tumultuous, tranquil, terrible, tragic, and terrific times, women have upheld our collective sense of humor: the moms and aunts, the sisters and cousins, wives and daughters, BFFs and girlfriends. Today we can add to that list a growing cast of perfect strangers—stand-up comics, improv artists, variety-hour and podcast hosts—with whom we spend time on the page, through our headphones, on silver and small screens, and at clubs and open mics. The ladies in our lives have kept us laughing and lifted us through good times, bad times, and times in between. ✳ Comedy can be a balm; it can be a coping mechanism; it can be a channel for information and empathy; it can be a teaching tool; it can be an icebreaker; it can be a bridge or a web. Comedy can be a common thread, weaving us closer together when things seem to be tearing apart. Keeping in mind the long history of the human condition, with all of its hilarity and heartbreak, this book collects a century's worth of women's experiences in the form of observations, musings, anecdotes, instructions, and notes from the field. Whether wisdom from the golden girls of yesteryear or from the mouths of (relative) babes, these quotes— in turn hilarious, droll, devastating, poignant, unrelentingly honest, and so comforting for the truths they corroborate and reveal— stay relevant and reflect our times while leaving us, if we're lucky, with a lesson learned, and often with an earned and earnest laugh. ✳ Now, I'll let the women speak for themselves—and get the last laugh—as they very well deserve to do.

—Barbara Darko

We all enter this world crying.

Laughter is something we have to learn.

Gina Barreca

My father was
a proctologist;
my mother was an
abstract artist.
That's how I view
the world.

Sandra Bernhard

It took me years to
realize that "normal" is
actually super boring
and that being myself
was harder, but infinitely
more rewarding.

Franchesca Ramsey

Normal is nothing more than a cycle on a washing machine.

Whoopi Goldberg

Everybody I know who is funny,

it's in them....

You have to be born to be born with a sense of humor and a sense of timing.

Carol Burnett

I didn't know about
stand-up as an art.
I just thought stand-up
comedians were
old men in suits talking
about their wives.

Natasha Leggero

There's never really nothing else I could do because it is my calling in life to entertain.

Luenell

My grandfather once said, having watched me one entire afternoon,

prancing and

leaping and cavorting,

"This child will either end up on stage or in jail."

Mary Tyler Moore

You create your own voice on your stage. And people think that it's very scary, but it's about me! I'm looking to be the center of attention, and I found it! I'm here!

Hana Mae Lee

I'm the youngest in my family and everyone is very funny, and I was always trying to keep up with them. I just loved making people laugh…. But I put it all away during high school and college. I thought, "That's not actually something you do with your life."

Lisa Kudrow

I remember our
first day in the theater
department at
UCLA, they told us,
"If there's anything
else you'd be happy
doing in your life,
do it, because this
is not an easy industry."
And, on some level,
that's true.

You really have to love it and not be able to live without it—

You'd be crazy

doing this without absolutely loving it.

Nasim Pedrad

Either they laugh or they laugh or they don't.

When I got into comedy, it scared me because [In theater] when you're onstage, you're not yourself and those aren't your words. When you're onstage as a comic, that's you, and those are your words. But your destiny's your destiny.

Dulcé Sloan

It's like asking a basketball player, "When did you first know you could probably nail a three-pointer?" Who knows?... Funny is hard to define. Is it instinct? Science? Luck?

Jen Kirkman

It's okay, guys—

I'm surprised I'm

a comedian, too!

Aparna Nancherla

There was no plan B. There were times when I had seven dollars to my name and was like, maybe I should get a job? And then I was like, *nah*.

Robin Thede

Nothing prompts creativity like poverty, a feeling of hopelessness, and a bit of panic.

Catherine Tate

The brief time that I did stand-up comedy, there was something about going onstage and failing miserably that…

just made me

feel so inspired.

Aubrey Plaza

I love stand-up so much, I've got an almost unhealthy relationship with it. Like, if I don't perform I get really depressed.

Josie Long

If I don't write something or perform… I feel like I haven't had enough water or enough to breathe.

Michelle Buteau

Stand-up keeps
you on your toes
because it's instant.
With TV and movies,
you have to wait
for the numbers
to come in to see
what happened
at the box office.
With stand-up, it's
right there, that
night, in your face.

Mo'Nique

When it's
going well,
stand-up
is the best
thing in the
world, but
when it's not,
it feels like
all your toes
are being

pulled off

one

by

one.

Jennifer Coolidge

People get hung up on writing smart shit. To me, it's more about performance. Lucille Ball and Moms Mabley, they had *face*. Before they even said a word, they made you crack up.

Leslie Jones

People go to a comedy show because comedy can go either way. . . . Because it is so raw. It's not TV. They can't put a laugh track in. You're out there.

Kristen Schaal

What is funny? Funny is subjective. Whatever feels most terrifying, I want to go to there.

Ilana Glazer

I often hunch over, or I get down really low, and it's not because I'm an old Yiddish storyteller; it's because if I could crawl inside

your brain and
give it a hug,

that's what
I want to do.

Iliza Shlesinger

Being onstage has this really great
effect, where you really don't think about
anything else that's going on in your life....
It's like an Adderall pill; you just have
to focus on making whatever you're doing
work, and making the audience enjoy it.

Jo Firestone

Accentuate the positives, medicate the negatives.

Amy Sedaris

I just prefer
to see the dark
side of things.
The glass is
always half empty.
And cracked.
And I just cut my
lip on it. And
chipped a tooth.

Janeane Garofalo

I don't thrive on misery, myself.
I mean, I've obviously created
during a time of misery, but I also
create from a place of joy.

Tig Notaro

It's actually really human to find
some levity in something that's heavy.
You'll talk to people, anyone really,
and for example they'll say something
like, "We were at this really sad
funeral, and then we got the giggles."
...That's really universal.

Maeve Higgins

Sometimes the only way to deal with horrific things in life is through a dark sense of humor.

Margaret Cho

Sometimes something seems dark, but within that darkness is a certain something wonderful that you can't see with your eyes.

Danitra Vance

I'm not afraid to make jokes at my own expense, and I've just found that makes people a little more comfortable and can open the door for people to feel a little bit more understanding and accepting of where you're coming from.

Franchesca Ramsey

I want to be a stand-up for everybody and tell stories that are relatable to everyone. And you can come to my show and forget about all the crazy stuff going on in life and just laugh, have a good time and not worry about anything.

44

Fortune Feimster

Bring your sense of humor with you at all times. Bring your friends with a sense of humor. If their friends have a sense of humor, invite them, too.

Gina Barreca

When I started talking about
[anxiety and depression]
I didn't really have an agenda.
It resonated with a lot of
people in a way I didn't think it
would, so it encouraged me
to keep talking about it.

Aparna Nancherla

I couldn't afford
therapy, so I just
watched *Frasier*.
Season four was
a breakthrough.

Cristela Alonzo

Part of my act is meant to shake
you up. It looks like I'm being funny,
but I'm reminding you of other things.
Life is tough, darling. Life is hard.
And we better laugh at everything,
otherwise we're going down the tube.

Joan Rivers

Entertainment
is company in this
desolate world.

Charlyne Yi

Entertainment is supposed to uplift and encourage and take people's minds off the garbage they're facing every day. I'm going to focus on that, and I'm going to focus on reminding people that love is what we're supposed to be doing with each other.

Yvette Nicole Brown

I think it's perfectly valid to go out and get laughs. I think it's a lovely thing to do actually, it's a lovely life-affirming job: you go out and you make people laugh. I think that's great. Who wouldn't want to do that?

Victoria Wood

As a stand-up,
I tried to change
the world.

As an entertainer,
I try to entertain.

And as a lesbian, I try to pick up the prettiest girl in the room.

Not necessarily in that order.

Lea DeLaria

What I hear from people is,
"Oh my God! You're Lori Beth!
You were such a big part of
my childhood." It's really nice.

Lori Beth Denberg

You'll say something and
be like, "That's going to be on
television? That's going to be on
someone's TV! That's ridiculous."
It's definitely really, really
cool and I feel really, really lucky.

Naomi Ekperigin

I love it when a woman hugs me. I love it when they say that I make them laugh because that means I'm doing what God called me to do…. My fans know my heart and they get it.

Sherri Shepherd

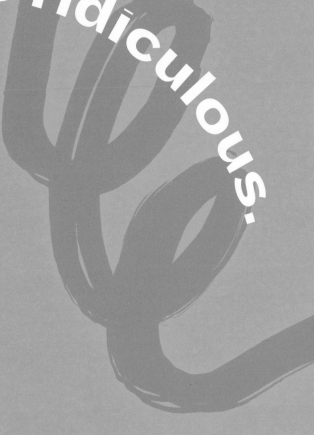

Everything I get to do is so ridiculous.

I can't believe I get to do this shit.

Amber Ruffin

Hollywood to me, I never get the real glamour and romance. I look at an old picture of Veronica Lake, you know, looking glamorous, and I just look at her and think, "Maybe she had her period that day."

Tracey Ullman

I will have one of the cleanest obits of any actress. I never did cheesecake like Ann Sheridan or Betty Grable. I just used my hair.

Veronica Lake

I've had the fame and the joy of getting laughter— those are gifts.

Mary Tyler Moore

Applause is almost a duty. Laughter is a reward.

Carol Channing

Fame changes a lot of things, but it can't change a light bulb.

Gilda Radner

I'm here, start the cameras!

Jane Lynch

We were shooting this glamorous scene
and I looked up and saw the office I got fired from.
I thought: "Oh my God, everything has come
full circle." I left that job in pursuit of Awkwafina.
And here I was shooting a scene with Rihanna.
Getting fired from that job really hurt my feelings.
Now I could just look up and say, "Fuck y'all."

Awkwafina

I told my bestie,
"I'm only two blocks away
from the 9000 building.
I'm very close to making it."
And my friend goes,
"You're in Times Square,
bitch. You made it."

Retta

I always
wanted to
be somebody,
but now
I realize
I should have
been more
specific.

Lily Tomlin

Every comic is really a frustrated rock star.

Alex Borstein

Of course I talk to myself.
I like a good speaker,
and I appreciate an
intelligent audience.

Dorothy Parker

I'm a very
low-key person
but for some
reason, I like
to act out.

Kate McKinnon

I don't set out
to offend or shock,
but I also don't do
anything to avoid it.

Sarah Silverman

I don't know if this is comedy,
but I really like getting
the audience all riled up.
That's my favorite thing.

Jo Firestone

Comedy should be explosive.

Jane Curtin

Any woman who can't say a four-letter word sometimes is deceitful.

Fanny Brice

I curse because I want to. It's just like putting hot sauce on chicken, it makes the meat taste better for some folks and others, not so much.

Sommore

I have now become beloved and iconic for telling people to go fuck themselves. For the rest of my life, that will be my legacy. It's fine. You could be known for worse.

Susie Essman

If I say the right thing, please excuse me.

Gracie Allen

As far as
I can tell,
comedians
are pretty
serious people,
and that's
why they
make fun of
things all
of the time.

Maria Bamford

Comedy, for me, was just being honest, and playing it for real. I've seen so many wonderful actors who turn into creatures from another planet when they're told they are supposed to be playing comedy.

Bea Arthur

Whatever comes natural is probably the truth, and the truth is the strongest form of anything—whether serious or funny.

Charlyne Yi

My idea as far as comedy goes has always been to push the limits of what's acceptable for a woman to do or say or be.

Lea DeLaria

When I'm good, I'm very good. When I'm bad, I'm better.

Mae West

Every woman wants to feel great about themselves. It's just nice to feel supported in that way, and it's what my live shows are about— just making women feel stronger, and better, and celebrating.

Bridget Everett

There's power in looking silly and not caring that you do.

Amy Poehler

[Writing a bit] is
a hell of a process....
It's like childbirth.
You don't remember
how hellish it is,
but you have fond
memories of the
product that came out.
I am assuming that
is how childbirth is.

Lisa Lampanelli

I think part of the problem
is that women, we're too cute
about what happens to our
bodies. When we have a baby,
we'll be like, "It's a miracle."
It's not a miracle, it's a natural
disaster. When Florida gets
hit with a hurricane, they
send supplies and help because
they tell you how bad it is.
They don't go, like, "And then
God kissed Florida with wind."
Before you know it, they'll
have concerts for your vagina.
Bono will be in there.

Michelle Wolf

Women have to push
harder, jump farther,
stay later, think better,
shit faster, all while
trying their best
to maintain whatever
society says today
their body should look
like, how they should
parent, what they
should wear, when
they should find love,
what's inappropriate

for them to do, say, be, feel, or fuck. The outward pressures are constant, but the inward congestion of doubts and insecurities are sometimes louder—

women really can have it all!

Abbi Jacobson

Confidence is 10 percent hard work and 90 percent delusion—just thinking foolishly that you will be able to do what you want to do.

Tina Fey

I have always wanted to be seen as
a great comedian, and when you throw
"woman" in front of it, it just makes me see
that you see me as some kind of freakish
subset. You don't say, "This is the funniest
male comedian." But it's this weird thing
that subtly indicates, "I don't see you
as really in the running on a comedy level."

Chelsea Peretti

Time for an exercise, which I shall call "Say It Out
Loud With Miranda." Please take a moment to sit back,
breathe and intone: "I am taking myself seriously
as a woman." Note your response. If you're reading
this on the bus, or surreptitiously in the cinema,
or in any other public scenario, then please note other
people's responses. (If you are male, and teenaged,
and reading this in a room with other teenage boys, then
for your own safety I advise you not to participate.)

Miranda Hart

I was a tomboy and a competitor, so when I got
in the world of comedy and brought my mouth with me,
people would say to me, "Well, you probably need
to tone it down. A lady can't be received in this way."
But I'd be damned if somebody is going to lecture
me on how to be a lady.…I had a lot of material
to shock and let people know not to fuck with me.
I'm a lady and I say what I want to say.

Adele Givens

I'd often refer to myself
as a "tomboy," until
I learned that liking
and watching sports
but not actually being
good at them does
not make you a tomboy,
it makes you a human.

Phoebe Robinson

Whenever I read a Reddit review of a female stand-up, it's always guys saying, "They just talk about their vaginas." It's such a double standard, because all men talk about is their dicks. . . . I think the problem here is just that women are talking.

Nikki Glaser

Who knows how many kinds of different things women would have done if they hadn't been told all this bullshit.

Rachel Feinstein

stop

telling girls
they can
be anything
they want
when they
grow up . . .
not because
they can't,

but because it would've

never occurred

to them they couldn't.

Sarah Silverman

For the first ten years
of my career as a
writer, I never worked
in another room with
a woman—it was all men.
I was referred to as
the "girl writer" in one
room for two years.
And when I was allowed
to speak, it was when
they had something the
female characters
were going to say. It is
torturous and awful.

Robin Thede

There is this resurgence
of amazing roles for women.
It's because TV is so good ...
it's upped the game in movies.

Molly Shannon

I learned the enormous
power of writing for
yourself, especially now
that people seem to be
receptive to the fact that
women can write.

Maya Rudolph

When I started, people
were basically like: "If you're
a woman onstage, you should
desex yourself. Don't wear
sexy clothes. Don't talk about
sex." And now when I see
Amy Schumer's popularity,
or Ali Wong—and these
are women that are wearing
dresses and they are talking
about their sex lives—I go,
"Oh, maybe I was kind of
internalizing too extreme of
an erasure of my gender."
So I've been quietly trying
to make sense of what it all
means for me.

Chelsea Peretti

I spent seven hours today at the beauty parlor; hell, that was just for the estimate.

Phyllis Diller

I often feel that with women, people look at you, but they don't really observe you. They look *past* you, they look *through* you, they look *at* you but they're not looking in your eyes or your soul. People are so unobservant of women and I think that we're smarter and we have more to say when we do it right. Female comics could take over this whole fucking game if they did it right.

85

Luenell

A certain kind
of exhaustion sets
in from having
to constantly
explain and justify
one's existence
or participation
in an artistic or
creative realm.
What a privilege
it must be to never
have to answer
the question.

Carrie Brownstein

I never want to be called the funniest
Indian female comedian that exists.
I feel like I can go head-to-head with
the best white, male comedy writers
that are out there. Why would I want
to self-categorize myself into a smaller
group than I'm able to compete in?

Mindy Kaling

It's hard for us to get stage time,
to even go up at open mics. I tell women
we need to hear your voice. I want
to see a woman who has six kids by
six different men. I want to see what
she thinks is funny. I want to see
her get up onstage and bare her soul.

Sommore

I don't feel equipped to go on a talk show [and speak about policy]. But what I do think I can do is I can write a fat character with dignity who's in control of her body and has humanity. And when I'm making my own show, I can make an effort to hire diverse people.

Aidy Bryant

You can put on
makeup to look Asian
or Latino or black,
but black, Asian and
Latino people know
you're not. And disabled
people watching their
disabilities being
poorly portrayed know
it's not them either.

Maysoon Zayid

Just being a visibly marginalized person and not addressing it in an artistic space is almost more political than for me to be onstage talking about it. It's fully a privilege to be an artist

and not have
to talk about your
oppression in
your art. If you
don't have that
challenge—

you get to make art
about a hoverboard!

Patti Harrison

People are so quick to praise men for avoiding vehemently bad behavior, whilst holding women to a million standards they'll never meet. It's like, "Oh, he didn't murder anyone? He's my hero."

Shelby Lorman

People ask me why I'm so hard on men. It's because they've gotten a really easy ride.

Chelsea Handler

You know how people are always like, "I wonder why there aren't more female comedians?" Maybe it's because every time a woman opens her mouth to tell a joke, someone tries to put their dick in it.

There are plenty of things in trying to stay alive in show business that are very similar to trying to stay alive politically. And being a woman, a middle-aged woman, trying to stay relevant and viable—I get it. Not being taken seriously. It's infuriating....One has to power through it. And frankly, I've made a career of playing unlikable people. I don't cotton to likability.

Julia Louis-Dreyfus

This isn't a bra,
it's body armor.
And this isn't makeup,
it's war paint.

Iliza Shlesinger

The first thing I do
in the morning is
brush my teeth and
sharpen my tongue.

Dorothy Parker

I've played many roles that were originally written for men. . . . I think people write authoritarian parts, sort of knee-jerk, as male. You know, he's the boss, he's this and that. And if you ask if it can be a woman, it's thinking outside the box.

Jane Lynch

It's acceptable for men to act the fool. When women try, they're considered aggressive and opinionated.

Madeline Kahn

Telling me to relax or smile when I'm angry is like bringing a birthday cake into an ape sanctuary.

You're just asking to get your nose and genitals bitten off.

Amy Poehler

I'm so irritated with this idea of men as gatekeepers.... I'm like, "Why is there a door here in general? Get out of my way, I'm trying to move forward!"

Jenny Slate

There are so many funny women in the world, and there [have] been for so many years, so I'll be happy when people can just move on from that, and things can just be "comedies" and not "female" or "male."

Kristen Wiig

I say if I'm beautiful. I say
if I'm strong. You will not
determine my story—I will.
I will speak and share and
fuck and love and I will never
apologize to the frightened
millions who resent that
they never had it in them to
do it. I stand here and I am
amazing, for you. Not because
of you. I am not who I sleep
with. I am not my weight.
I am not my mother. I am
myself. And I am all of you.

Amy Schumer

There's this idea of the "Angry Black Woman," and ... I often feel like I'm put in that category. A lot of women of color are put in that category, when I think our anger is justified. I actually think that female anger isn't that different from male anger. Boxing and football are, like, national fucking pastimes. And yet, when a woman expresses that she is unhappy with the way in which our society exists, that's a big fucking problem. That's crazy to me.

Jessica Williams

The sassy black woman trope—
I don't think it's a black thing....
The gold standard for sass
for me is Bea Arthur, and she
was a white woman. I have
always been frustrated by
the idea that a white woman
can be sassy and that would
not define her, but black
women are stamped with that,
and that's something that's
expected of us. Everyone can
be sassy. Everyone can be
frustrated or fed up or joyful.

Yvette Nicole Brown

In high school and college, the only representation of black women I saw was on reality television. And so to have this renaissance—to be alongside so many amazing content creators and actors of color—feels very optimistic. We're so aware of what it's like to not have those images; we're clinging on to them.

Issa Rae

Those girls [from Broad City] thanked me when I did the show for paving the way so that they could do what they do today. I never really thought about it in that context and it really made me so happy.

Fran Drescher

I love when I do my stand-up shows that the audience is so diverse: younger, older, men, women, goth Mexican kids, Asian bros. It's not that I'm exactly like them, but it's nice to have somebody out there tell you it's okay to be exactly yourself.

Aisha Tyler

The narrative in the mainstream media about [indigenous women] is always so serious, and the world doesn't see our funny side. And the world deserves to see our funny side; we're really funny.

Adrianne Chalepah

I'm proud to
carry that torch
and be like
"I'm gay! I'm black!
Hang your
dreams on me.
Hang your
hopes on me.
I'll carry them
to the best
of my ability."

Lena Waithe

[Marginalization] is what breeds creativity, it's what inspires us. I can't be mad about it because I'm black, I'm dark and I'm fucking beautiful. My skin is gorgeous, I love myself, people with good eyesight love me too, and the rest of the world can fuck themselves.

Michaela Coel

I recently became vegan because I felt that as a Jewish lesbian, I wasn't part of a small enough minority. So now I'm a Jewish lesbian vegan.

Carol Leifer

I always want to remind folks when they talk about how exciting it is that, "Oh, these voices are coming from nowhere." It's, like, no, these voices were silenced. These voices were here and folks were out there doing the work and selling tickets and being funny and those in the mainstream were opting out of listening.

Cameron Esposito

Every black comedian in the country knew what I could do. But that doesn't mean everyone else is paying attention.

Leslie Jones

I used to get criticisms like: "All she talks about is being black." No, I don't. I talk about me. The fact that I'm a black woman is what you're seeing.

Gina Yashere

We need to raise up the talents of people from all backgrounds. We have to give them chances and opportunities instead of the one door that opens for them to be the quirky sidekick. We only see the black or Asian friend who, apparently, only has white friends. That's not real—at all. I'm looking to get in a position where I can change that.

Kulap Vilaysack

Funny is funny, and it can come in eight billion different shades and flavors.

109

Melissa McCarthy

"Why the fuck

not me?"

should be your motto.

Mindy Kaling

Any narrative about immigration is very vital. . . . More people are covering immigrant stories and giving immigrants a platform for their voices, which is so needed. If you actually care about something and believe in it, it's not crazy and it's not corny to just keep pushing.

Maeve Higgins

I love and am very proud of my Iranian heritage. It's shaped who I am as a performer, and if I ever poke fun at it, it's coming from a place of love.

Nasim Pedrad

If people can laugh
and think critically, in lieu
of outright judgment,
that's an effective loophole
to get people talking.

Shelby Lorman

If people are laughing, they're listening.

Naomi Ekperigin

Here are some ground rules
for social justice comedy.
First off, it's not partisan, OK?
This isn't political comedy.
This is about justice, and no one
is against justice. Two, it's
inviting and warm. It makes you
feel like you're sitting inside
of a burrito. Three, it's funny,
but sneaky. Like, you could
be hearing a—like an interesting
treatise on income inequality
that's encased in a really
sophisticated poop joke.

Negin Farsad

Mind blowing that entertainers are held to a higher standard than our president.

Deanna MAD

Diversity makes for better art and entertainment. You know who said that? Barack Obama. You know who doesn't have time to talk about the hiring practices in Hollywood because he's really busy with wars and the economy and stuff? Barack Obama. Things must be pretty bad when the president has to step in and say, "Maybe you guys should try to include everyone?"

Sasheer Zamata

I don't want to be in a relationship.
I don't want to be in a relationship for
the same reason I don't want a kid.
I don't want anything in my life to be
more important than me. And maybe
that's selfish and mean, but the jig is up:
I'm not a nice lady.

Michelle Wolf

DIY stands for
"you should've
married someone
with more money."

Ali Wong

I really just got married for the material, to tell you the truth.

Anjelah Johnson

The desire to get married is a basic and primal instinct in women. It's followed by another basic and primal instinct: the desire to be single again.

Nora Ephron

For guys, sex is like
going to a restaurant,
and no matter what you
order off that menu,
you walk out of there going,
"Damn, that was good!"…
Women, it doesn't work
like that for us. We go
to the restaurant and order
something. Sometimes
it's good. Sometimes you
gotta send it back.

Wanda Sykes

I blame my mother for my poor sex life. All she told me was, "The man goes on top and the woman underneath." For three years my husband and I slept in bunk beds.

Joan Rivers

I think husbands and wives should live in separate houses. If there's enough money, the children should live in a third.

Cloris Leachman

I always loved children and babies and knew I wanted them, so being a mum came easily to me. I speak to my kids on a regular basis. I know their names. I even hug them occasionally.

Victoria Wood

Advice to children crossing the street: damn the lights. Watch the cars. The lights ain't never killed nobody.

Jackie "Moms" Mabley

Imagine for a moment playing by children's rules. If you were at a party and saw someone you liked, you could just go and hold their hand. If they then try to kiss you and you don't like it, you can push them over. If your aunty gives you a Christmas present that you're not too keen on, you can throw it back in her face and burst into tears. You can gallop freely. You can skip. Children have got it right. The tragedy is, none of this is permissible as an adult. Although one thing surely is—and I'll bet you know what I'm going to say—that's right, the galloping. Such fun!

Miranda Hart

Adults are always asking little kids what they want to be when they grow up because they're looking for ideas.

Paula Poundstone

We are always growing up. I'm growing up as I type this. An eighty-seven-year-old woman is still technically growing up. So be as immature as you want. Right now, you are the youngest you're ever going to be.

Mamrie Hart

There are so many things I won't live long enough to find out about, but I'm still curious about them. You know people who are already saying, "I'm going to be thirty—oh, what am I going to do?" Well, use that decade! Use them all!

Betty White

Middle age is when you finally get your shit together and your ass falls apart.

Lily Tomlin

The only parts left of my original body are my elbows.

Phyllis Diller

Our faces are lies and our necks are the truth. You have to cut open a redwood tree to see how old it is, but you wouldn't if it had a neck.

127

Nora Ephron

I have a two-story house and a bad memory, so I'm up and down those stairs all the time. That's my exercise.

Betty White

Yoga is Simon Says
for adults who have
lotsa free time.

Ali Wong

This is how bad
I am at working out:
I've got a personal
trainer and *he's*
getting fat.

Gina Yashere

I went on a
seven-day diet
once. I ate it
all in one day.

Estelle Getty

I've been on a
diet for two weeks
and all I've lost
is two weeks.

Totie Fields

The secret of staying young is to live honestly, eat slowly, and lie about your age.

Lucille Ball

I've told so many lies about my age I don't know how old I am myself.

Ruby Wax

If I had
to live my
life again,
I'd make
the same
mistakes,

only sooner.

Tallulah Bankhead

Between two evils, I generally like to pick the one I never tried before.

Mae West

I'm still me.
But [my act]
has become way
more honest.
When you get
older you're like
"Eh, what do
I have to lose?
Whatever."

Wanda Sykes

I used to [impersonate] everyone in my village and everyone at school and everyone in the news, and I'm still doing that same show. I'm now fifty-six. I think I can do it in my eighties. I'll just, you know, impersonate everyone around me then in the nursing home.

Tracey Ullman

I've always hung out with people older than me, and they make life look good— like aging is something to strive for. My grandmother died at ninety-four with all her faculties and her sense of humor intact. Never think you can't start something new because of your age.

Queen Latifah

My grandmother started walking five miles a day when she was sixty. She's ninety-seven now, and we don't know where the hell she is.

Ellen DeGeneres

The thing I'm most excited about is women in comedy being such a normal thing that no one's surprised by it anymore.

And, I feel like we're way past needing to prove that that can be done.

Nasim Pedrad

1918

Dorothy Parker cofounds the Algonquin Round Table, a circle of notable writers and wisecrackers. A writer herself, Parker brought her caustic wit to bear in poetry and criticism.

1921

Jackie "Moms" **Mabley** comes out as one of the first openly gay comedians at the age of twenty-seven. She was the first female comic to perform at the Apollo, in 1930, and at Carnegie Hall, in 1962.

1931

Actress **Tallulah Bankhead** has her Hollywood break in *Tarnished Lady*. She previously achieved success as a stage actress, earning an international reputation for her flamboyance, wit, and verve.

1935

Paramount Pictures star **Mae West** becomes the highest-paid movie star— and by some accounts, the second-highest-paid person in the United States, after newspaperman William Randolph Hearst.

1969

Lily Tomlin gets her television break as a newcomer on the sketch comedy show *Rowan & Martin's Laugh-In*.

1938

Fanny Brice, known for her theater, burlesque, radio, and film roles, and immortalized in the semibiographical film *Funny Girl*, stars in *My Man*, becoming the first woman lead in a motion picture with sound. Brice was later dubbed "America's first female comedy superstar."

1951

I Love Lucy, starring **Lucille Ball**, airs on CBS. For four seasons, it was the most-watched television show in The United States.

1975

Saturday Night Live airs on NBC with members **Jane Curtin**, **Gilda Radner**, and **Laraine Newman**.

1985

Whoopi Goldberg is nominated for an Academy Award for Best Actress for her role as Celie in *The Color Purple*.

1994

Margaret Cho becomes the first Asian American to receive an American Comedy Award, clinching the title Best Female Stand-Up Comic. An activist, Cho has advocated for the legalization of gay marriage in the United States and other progressive reforms.

1999

Tina Fey becomes the first female lead writer on *SNL*. Her sitcom *30 Rock* took the Emmy for Outstanding Comedy Series from 2007–2010.

2004

Wanda Sykes is ranked on *Entertainment Weekly*'s list of "25 Funniest People in America."

2016

Samantha Bee becomes the first woman to host her own late-night show on a major TV network with *Full Frontal*.

2015

Shaina Stigler and **Natalie Wall** host Bad Assery, the first Women and Comedy Conference, at Littlefield in Brooklyn, New York.

2014

Amber Ruffin is hired to write for *Late Night with Seth Meyers*, becoming the first-ever black, female late-night television writer.

2019

Robin Thede's *A Black Lady Sketch Show* premieres on HBO—the first sketch comedy series created by, written by, produced by, and starring a cast of black women.

100 Years of Women in Comedy

142

Index

Funniest comedian in the game, not just woman. I hate that shit.

Leslie Jones